# digital wellness

*Your Playbook for ~~Surviving~~ **Thriving** in the Remote Work Era*

By Amy Blankson, MBA and Nina Hersher, MSW

Digital Wellness Institute

# Table of Contents


**LEARNING TO FLOURISH IN THE DIGITAL ERA** .......................................... **3**
    A Duty of Care.................................................................. 4
    Redefining Wellness for the Digital Era............................. 4
    Digital Flourishing® ......................................................... 5

**DISTRACTION AND THE ATTENTION ECONOMY** ...................................... **7**

**MARKET TRENDS: THE NEW VIRTUAL WORKPLACE** ................................ **9**

**ASSESSING AND ADDRESSING DIGITAL WELLNESS** ................................ **12**

**PLAYBOOK FOR EMPLOYEES** .............................................................. **15**
    Strategy #1: Ground Yourself ......................................... 16
    Strategy #2: Create a Habitat for Happiness .................. 18
    Strategy #3: Optimize Your Habits .................................. 20

**PLAYBOOK FOR TEAMS** ....................................................................... **24**
    Strategy #1: Write a Communication Charter.................. 25
    Strategy #2: Encourage Downtime.................................. 28
    Strategy #3: Foster Authentic Engagement - Both Online and Offline ............... 29

**TAKEAWAYS AND NEXT STEPS:**
**CREATING A POSITIVE DIGITAL CULTURE AT WORK** ................................ **31**

**GLOSSARY** ...................................................................................... **33**

**ADDITIONAL RESOURCES** .................................................................. **35**

**ABOUT THE AUTHORS** ....................................................................... **36**

**ABOUT THE ORGANIZATIONS** ............................................................. **37**

**REFERENCES** ................................................................................... **38**

# Learning to Flourish in the Digital Era

**Click. Pause... Scroll. Repeat.**

This is the pattern that fills 38 percent of our waking hours. Since the pandemic began, the average time spent on screens has jumped from four to six hours per day. And the fallout from this increased time spent online is far-reaching. In a recent survey conducted by OnePoll, nearly six in 10 respondents said they experience screen-related aches and pains, causing them to feel physically drained and less productive. Yet, two-thirds of respondents said that the first thing they do in the morning is turn to their phone.

Research confirms that large amounts of <u>unfocused time online can fuel feelings of anxiety and increase the risk of depression</u>. Many people within the workforce are living out that reality right now, as COVID-19 has placed an exceptional strain on employees, with many <u>spending over half of their day on connected devices</u>, working remotely amidst constant uncertainty.

It's time that we take control of this unfocused time. A survey conducted by <u>Monster.com</u> in July 2020 found that over two-thirds of employees are experiencing burnout symptoms while working from home (a 20 percent increase since May). While this statistic is alarming, it is not that surprising given that 55 percent of them are still checking their email after 11 p.m. We can do better, but employees need help to be at their best.

> **Digital Wellness** is no longer a luxury in the workplace; it is a business and lifestyle imperative for organizational performance.

Digital Wellness Institute

## A DUTY OF CARE

Today, <u>83 percent of employees</u> are looking to their employers for guidance in navigating the pressures of remote work. Yet many employers feel ill-equipped to deal with these new pressures.

That's why we wrote this Digital Wellness Playbook—to provide you with actionable, research-based guidance to support your employees, reclaim their attention, and act with full intention. Encouraging a positive digital culture can raise productivity and engagement rates, improve retention and recruitment, deepen employee and customer loyalty, and increase employee well-being overall.

**83%** of employees are looking to their employers for guidance in navigating the pressures of remote work.

## REDEFINING WELLNESS FOR THE DIGITAL ERA

For years, corporate wellness efforts have focused almost exclusively on mental and physical health, offering seminars and platforms to help employees reduce stress while improving in the areas of exercise, sleep, and happiness. Organizations spend vast amounts of time and resources tracking these indicators because they know that engagement scores have a direct impact on the bottom line.

These kinds of approaches, as well as benefits and perks, can certainly help buoy morale. However, employers can actually have a much deeper and often overlooked opportunity: upskilling employees to help them achieve Digital Wellness and strive toward meeting their potential.

**So what exactly is Digital Wellness?**
Digital Wellness is the optimum state of health and well-being that each individual using technology is capable of achieving.

# DIGITAL FLOURISHING®

To help you understand the different parts of Digital Wellness, we at the Digital Wellness Institute partnered with academic institutions across North America to create the Digital Flourishing® model, an empowerment-oriented approach to building positive digital practices into your life across the eight dimensions of Digital Wellness: productivity, environment, communication, relationships, mental health, physical health, the quantified self, and digital citizenship.

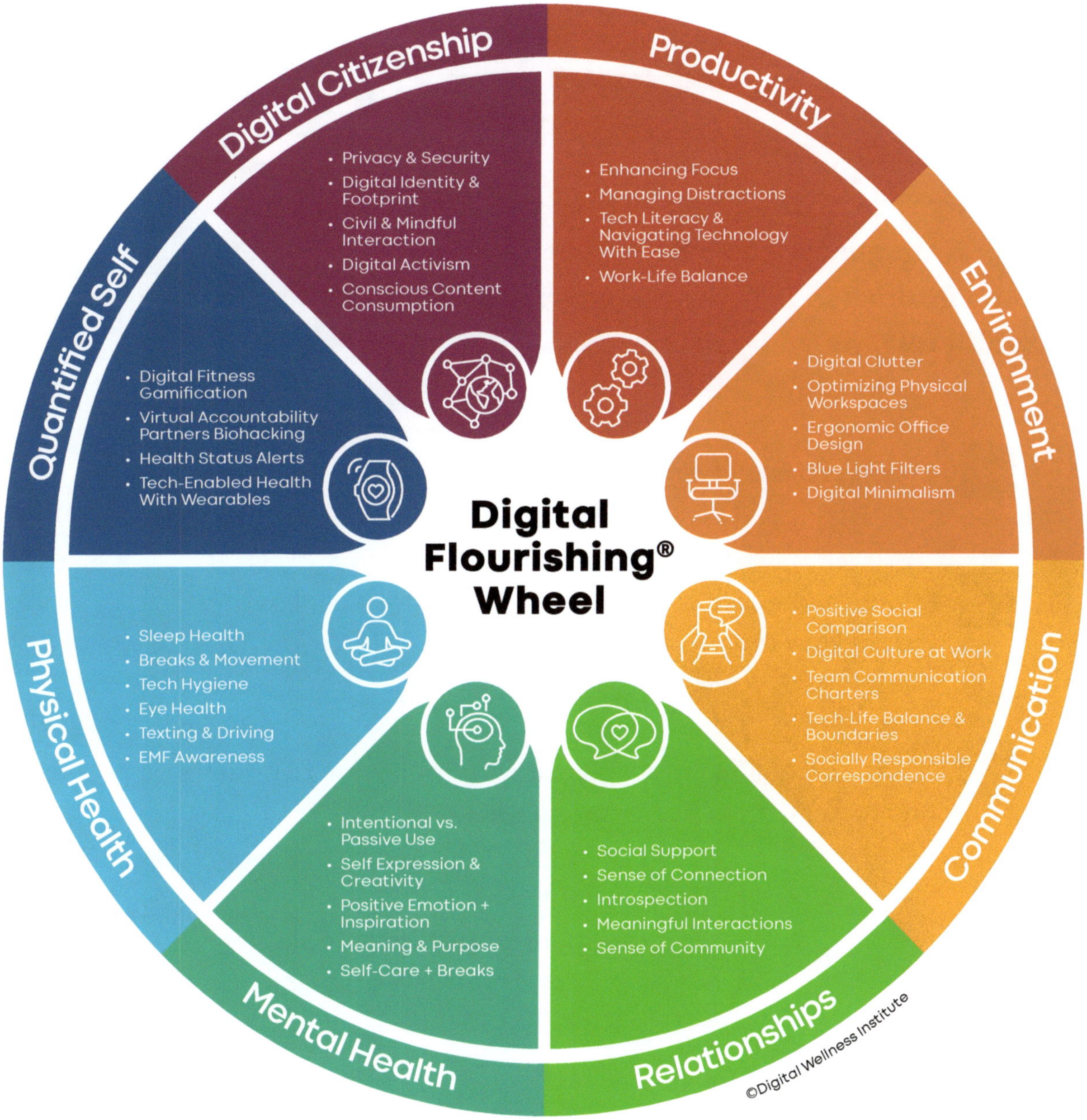

The goal of this model is to help individuals and organizations assess wellness in different domains of their lives, recognizing that many of the areas are interconnected. For instance, if we lean too heavily into improving productivity, our relationships might suffer. Or if we spend too long communicating on our devices, our physical health might fall by the wayside. This visual helps individuals constantly evaluate the shifting pressures in our world and recalibrate to find a better sense of balance.

**This playbook is designed to give you actionable guidance to help your teams flourish in the remote work era. Specifically, we will help you to:**

- ✓ **Create a positive digital culture within your organization.**

- ✓ **Effectively assess and address your Digital Wellness and that of your team.**

- ✓ **Write a communication charter with your team to optimize and foster authentic engagement.**

- ✓ **Support your employees with exercises for establishing effective digital boundaries and creating/breaking habits.**

# Distraction and the Attention Economy

Can I have your undivided attention? If you are reading this playbook in between checking your emails and scrolling through endless WhatsApp messages on your phone, you probably aren't alone! In fact, since the pandemic began in February, searches for "how to get your brain to focus" have increased 300 percent.

Connected device time has increased 46 percent over the past year, with the average individual spending 3 hours and 15 minutes each day on their smartphone. Research shows that once you pick up your phone, you have a 50 percent chance of picking up your phone a second time within the next three minutes.

While technology can be a boon for both productivity and connectivity, poor digital boundaries can turn devices into compulsions, rather than tools of efficiency. For instance, 67 percent of smartphone users compulsively check their phone for messages, alerts, or calls - even when they don't notice their phone ringing or vibrating.

Former Google Design Ethicist Tristan Harris explains that phones operate like clever slot machines, offering variable rewards highly attuned to hijack our attention and desires. In the recent Netflix documentary _The Social Dilemma_, Harris warns about the rise of the so-called "attention economy": an internet

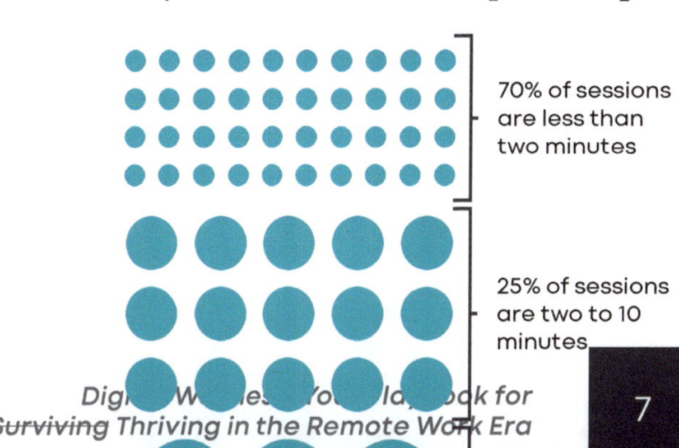

that was shaped around advertising to maximize page views, effectively turning our attention into a commodity to be bought and sold. Our devices are burgeoning with content we know we shouldn't look at, but we lack the self-control to fend off technology that is designed to prey on our individual human needs and desires.

But that doesn't have to be the end of the story. While it's easy for technology to disrupt our best intentions, ultimately we have human agency about when, where, why and how often we choose to engage with our devices.

Now is the time to utilize our human agency to create a positive digital culture. Let's take it back and optimize our time.

# Market Trends: The New Virtual Workplace

Since the pandemic erupted, we've witnessed a digital revolution, with a shift to remote work, e-learning, virtual teaching, and more digital access to services than ever before. According to McKinsey & Company, the world has leaped five years forward in consumer and business digital adoption in a matter of just a few weeks. More than 90 percent of executives expect the fallout from Covid-19 to fundamentally change the way they do business over the coming five years, with almost as many highlight the lasting impact the pandemic will have on customer behavior and needs.

Executives, community leaders, and educators across the country are facing new challenges - communicating in real-time with remote teams, emphasizing focus and productivity, decreasing churn, and increasing engagement - all while facing unprecedented levels of stress, anxiety, and uncharted territory.

The shift to remote work and education has accelerated interest in optimizing digital habits. In fact, 83 percent of employees are looking to their employer to help them find better balance. Here are the emerging trends that employers need to know to prepare for the new future of work:

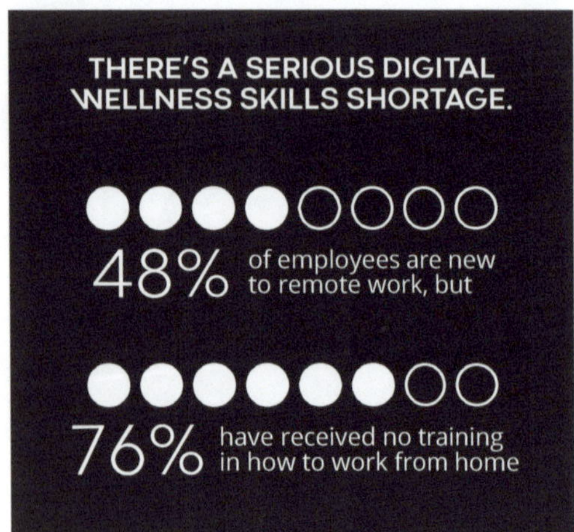


## THERE'S A WELLNESS CRISIS LOOMING.

**50%** reported **new aches and pains** since lockdown

**46%** **felt isolated** working from home during COVID-19

**36%** were concerned about the long-term effects on their **mental health**

**61%** have **not had a good conversation** with their manager about mental health during lockdown

## THERE'S AN OPPORTUNITY TO RETHINK HOW WE DO WORK.

**75%** of employees want to continue working from home more post-pandemic, with

**69%** wanting to work from home for most of the working week

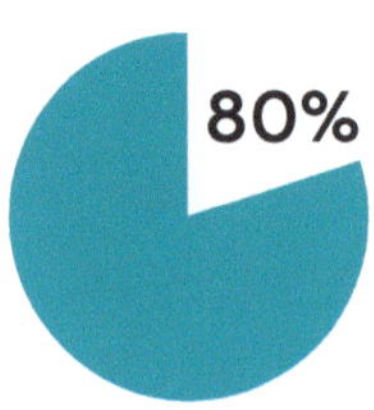


**80%** of remote workers report **less stress** when working from home

*Remote workers are **3.2 times more likely** to be more productive if they feel satisfied with their social connectivity.*

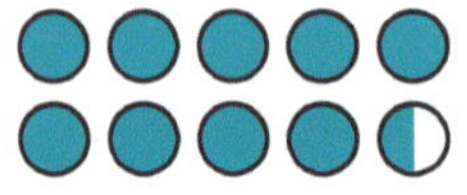
**94%**

of employees would potentially stay longer with a company that invests in learning and development.

Making time for learning is crucial. The average employee is only given ***24 minutes a week*** set aside for learning.

## THERE'S AN EXPONENTIAL SHIFT TOWARDS DISTANCE LEARNING.

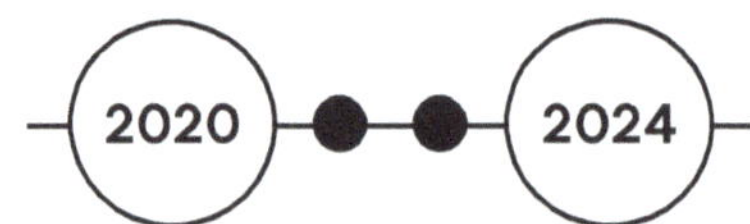


Between 2020 and 2024, **the online education industry is forecasted to grow at a CAGR rate of 13%,** far exceeding the expected market share of $350 billion that was predicted before the pandemic.

## THERE'S A NEED TO TRAIN WORKERS IN DIGITAL WELLNESS PRACTICES.

**51%** of chief human resource officers (CHROs) identify employee **anxiety and burnout as a top challenge** for their businesses, since the pandemic began.

**60%** of CHROs **plan to increase support** for well-being and mental health for their workforce in 2021.

**61%** of CHROs plan to implement initiatives that **increase workforce productivity** in 2021.

As a result of these trends, the way people receive
their education is evolving, both inside and outside the
workplace. More and more individuals are upskilling
online to meet the demands of the new working world,
to compete as a job-seeker in a time of economic
uncertainty, and even to change careers entirely after
this disruptive period. However, in order to be successful
in these pursuits, we need to train employees in
strategies for maximizing focus, setting effective digital
boundaries, and optimizing wellness.

# Assessing and Addressing Digital Wellness

How do you know if you and your employees are digitally flourishing? And in what ways can you quantitatively and qualitatively improve Digital Wellness?

Think of Digital Wellness as a spectrum, ranging from excessive technology use to complete unplugging. The goal of the Digital Wellness Institute is to help individuals flourish by finding a healthy balance for living with technology, rather than escaping from it.

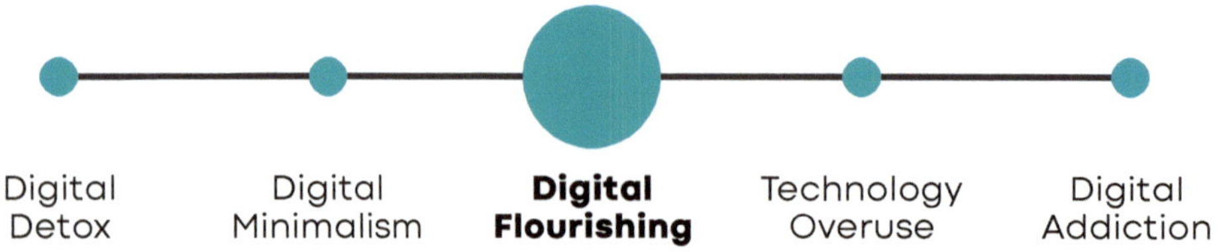


Assessing Digital Wellness is not just a matter of adding up screen time; rather, it is a holistic assessment that measures the impact of technology upon each of the eight domains in the Digital Flourishing® wheel.

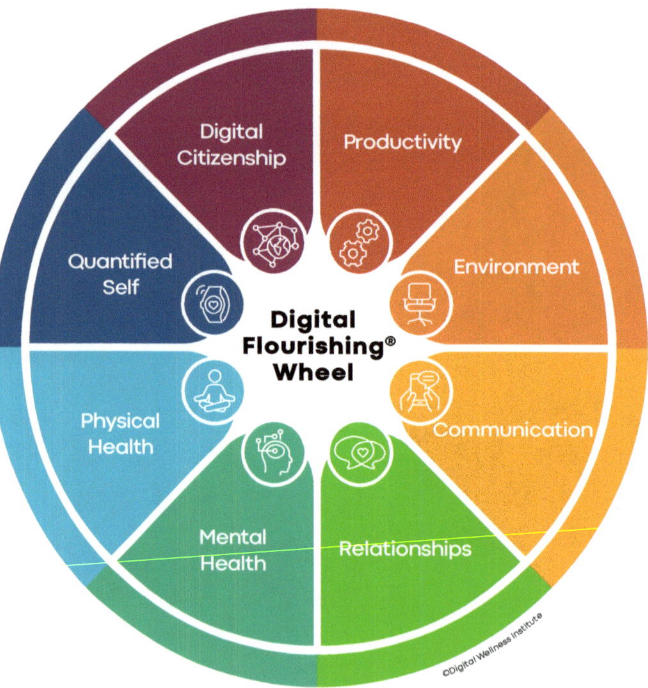

Most subjective assessments (i.e., questionnaires) in the space of Digital Wellness are clinical tools designed to draw on the problematic ways in which people use and are impacted by technology (e.g., measuring <u>internet addiction</u>, <u>social media disorders</u>, or <u>problematic smart-phone use</u>). While these tools are helpful in identifying the negative parts of technology use, they fail to capture the potential upside of technology engagement and overall wellness. As important as it is to quantify the problems created by distraction or inefficiency, it is equally important to underscore the ways that technology helps employees to thrive (e.g. by connecting with colleagues, facilitating upskilling and education, contributing to workplace productivity, and connecting employees with virtual resources for well-being.

Assessing Digital Wellness is important because it gives employers a more relevant and accurate snapshot of employee well-being, taking into consideration numerous factors (like feelings of angst around constant connectivity, digital overwhelm, and physical ailments) that do not show up on traditional engagement surveys, yet play silent but significant roles.

To address this need, the Digital Wellness Institute created the first-ever assessment tool called the Digital Flourishing survey®[1], which measures Digital Wellness across the eight domains of Digital Wellness.

Assessing people's level of Digital Flourishing® allows leaders to see where they can work on improving the teams' flourishing. Quantitative and qualitative measures give team members a great anchor upon which to improve. Focusing on digital flourishing instead of technology struggles in turn has a great motivational effect for the individual and teams in general as it helps to focus on the best possible teams and results.

To access this free tool, visit digitalflourishing.com and receive actionable tips for raising your overall Digital Wellness.

[1] *The Digital Flourishing® survey is currently being scientifically validated by a team of international researchers, led by Dr. Sophie Janicke-Bowles of Chapman University.*

# Playbook for Employees

To overcome, or at least counter-balance, the effects of the attention economy, employers can help employees to create a positive digital culture by teaching these strategies:

 Strategy #1: Ground Yourself

 Strategy #2: Create a Habitat for Happiness

 Strategy #3: Optimize Your Habits

# STRATEGY #1: GROUND YOURSELF

Digital Wellness is not simply about unplugging for periods of time; it's a holistic way of thinking about how, when, where and why we are interacting with technology and what the effects of those choices might be on other aspects of our health. It's about giving intention to our attention.

In the same way that the third prong on a plug helps to channel energy and prevent shock, taking a moment to ground our time online can help us to feel more balanced and fulfilled. By taking the time to examine what we are paying attention to and the quality of that attention when using our devices, we are better able to pause between stimulus and response, reduce reactive responding, and avoid going down Internet "rabbit holes" or compulsively checking email. An intentional approach allows us to have greater control over our digital device use without feeling like they control us.

Taking a moment to think about what drives and motivates you (e.g. loved ones, productivity, knowledge, relevance, faith, power, happiness, well-being, health). In the chart below, write down your top five values. Then, open the settings on your smartphone (for Apple, go to Settings>Screen Time; for Android, go to Settings>Digital Wellness) and write down the top five most used apps and the average amount of time spent on each.

| Top 5 Values | Top 5 Most Used Apps | Average Time Spent |
|---|---|---|
|  |  |  |
|  |  |  |
|  |  |  |
|  |  |  |
|  |  |  |

Do your values align with how you are spending your time? If not, don't despair. The goal of this exercise is to increase your awareness of your digital behaviors and the implicit time trade-offs that are happening. Digital Wellness is not about tech shaming, but rather about helping you to make better use of your time and energy. If you notice a misalignment, reset by taking a moment to write down your intentions for the coming week.

**Example of an intention to use technology less:** This week, I will play **Candy Crush** (most used app) less to be more **productive** (your value).

**Example of an intention to use technology better:** This week, I will login to **Duolingo** (least used app) at least three times a week to **work on my French** (your goal).

Research shows that by writing down your intention, you are 40% more likely to achieve your goal. Great job on taking the first step!

# STRATEGY #2: CREATE A HABITAT FOR HAPPINESS

Our smartphones enable - and encourage - continuous connection and, as such, they are continuously at our fingertips. While connection might be good in the right circumstances, the temptation to get distracted from important tasks is high. Even brief moments of task switching can cause you to lose as much as <u>40 percent of your productivity</u>. Stopping to read a text message might only take you 2.2 seconds, but in this span of time, you double your error rates on basic tasks.

<u>A recent study</u> found that, even when you are successfully ignoring your smartphone while concentrating on work, the mere presence of your device next to you reduces cognitive capacity by up to 10 percent. Why? Because your brain is actually anticipating that it might get a message and devotes resources to the potential message, rather than staying focused on the task at hand.

So what's the solution? Learning to live with technology - not just escape from it - means creating invisible fences, or digital boundaries, between our minds and our devices during periods of time where we want to be fully present. One simple strategy is to put your phone on do not disturb and tuck it behind your computer screen when you're working. This keeps your phone out of sight - eliminating those visual triggers that encourage compulsive checking - but still within reach should you need it. You may not be able to control for every distraction in your environment, but setting digital boundaries helps you to maximize your focus.

Another challenge of remote work is managing other household members who may not understand your work hours or habits. Here's a secret: post your schedule on your door, so that others can see when you are busy and when you are available. Your schedule may be clear in your mind, but others may not understand your flow of work. If you have a child, spouse, or roommate who is always interrupting or asking when you will be done with work, what they are really asking is when you will be available to engage with them. Communicate when you expect to be done with work or when you will be taking a break to minimize this type of interruption.

These subtle changes will make a world of difference.

| | |
|---|---|
| **C** | Clear your desk and your inbox. Physical clutter and digital clutter affect mental clarity and productivity. |
| **L** | Lift your computer to avoid tech tension. Invest in ergonomic solutions to stop hunching over your screen. A simple, adjustable laptop stand and supportive chair will promote better posture. Your body will thank you later! |
| **E** | Eliminate distractions. Create an unplugged box that doubles as an out-of-sight home for your phone - a drawer in a desk or any box will do! |
| **A** | Activate a dedicated workspace in your home. No office? No problem! Invest in a simple room divider to claim a corner of your home just for work. Differentiating spaces helps your brain with the division of "work" and "home" activities. Consider utilizing a space with natural light to boost your mood. |
| **R** | Refresh your office or desk by adding a plant. From low maintenance succulents to flowers that require daily care - there's a plant for everyone. A recent Japanese study found that people who kept a small plant on their desk had lower levels of anxiety and stress at the end of a four-week period. Copious research exists to support the idea that nature can serve as an antidote to overwhelm, overstimulation and "attention fatigue," as well enhance cognitive performance. |

***Diversity Equity & Inclusion Note:** When making recommendations, keep in mind that members of your team have differing work-from-home environments. While some have a dedicated home office with lots of natural light, others may be working at a kitchen table in a smaller, city apartment.

**Takeaway:** Remember, it's not about the size of your workspace but rather how you use it to create a habitat for happiness!

# STRATEGY #3: OPTIMIZE YOUR HABITS

Our lives revolve around habits. Research tells us approximately 43 percent of our behaviors each day are the result of ingrained habits. Some move us closer to our goals, while others lead us away from our goals.

It is often our tendency to want to change quite a few habits very quickly (think New Year's resolutions). But most goals are abandoned within weeks or even days because we don't understand the science behind habit formation, and therefore approach them with a flawed plan.

## THE THREE MYTHS OF HABIT CHANGE

### Myth #1: Habits are formed in 21 days

The leading research on habit formation tells us it takes an average of three times that long, 66 days, for a new habit to stick. So you shouldn't expect results for at least two months.

### Myth #2: Rewards are motivating

Do you think a fancy trip will motivate you to get into shape? Think again. Rewards may sound like a great idea, but unfortunately they aren't terribly effective at long-term behavior change because we have a tendency to stop the behavior once we receive the reward.

### Myth #3: Information leads to transformation

No matter how many self-help books you read, knowledge doesn't necessarily transfer into action because of something called the Information-Action Fallacy Trap. Information appeals to your "executive brain" (prefrontal cortex which processes logic), but emotions appeal to your "lizard brain" (basal ganglia and brainstem which process your primitive drives and habits). Your brain is constantly weighing these different responses, and often, we revert to our "lizard brains", which is why cigarette smokers, well-aware of the health risks, keep smoking.

To increase the odds of creative positive habit change, you need to get the "lizard" and the "executive brains" to work together. Our next section will teach you how!

### Start Small

BJ Fogg at the Behavior Design Lab at Stanford University says the <u>first big rule is to start small</u>. He calls them tiny steps, but others, such as Thrive Global founder Arianna Huffington, refer to them as micro-steps. They are the same thing. Small changes are less likely to frighten the "lizard brain" and if you stick to them, they become big changes over time.

### Stack Habits

Whether you realize it or not, you are a bundle of good habits, and you can leverage the good ones to create more good habits. James Clear, author of _Atomic Habits_, calls this "habit stacking." Perhaps you want to remove your smartphone from your room at night so it is not the first thing you look at in the morning? Pair that behavior with something else you do at bedtime, such as brushing your teeth or putting out your clothes for the next day. Once they become paired, your new habit gets to piggyback off the more ingrained habit.

### Reduce Friction

If you want to create a new habit, make it as easy as possible by reducing both the amount of friction and the number of decisions. When positive psychology expert and author <u>Shawn Achor</u> decided to start an exercise habit, he created a plan to improve the likelihood of success. Each evening, he decided what type of exercise he would do the next day. He then slept in his gym clothes and kept his gym shoes next to the bed. Each of these steps reduced the friction and amount of activation energy needed to fulfill his plan.

# STRATEGIES FOR BREAKING BAD HABITS

We've given you some tips for creating new habits, but what about breaking the old ones? Perhaps you engage in doom scrolling for hours before bedtime, only to feel depressed and not sleep well. How do you stop this if you've been doing it for a long time?

Habit expert Charles Duhigg says the best way to address an undesirable habit is to follow the Golden Rule of Habit Change. Our habits are typically part of a 3-step process: trigger, routine, reward. Breaking the chain is extremely difficult because it has a neural pathway in the brain that never completely goes away, even with time, so rather than trying to break the chain, just switch out the undesirable routine.

So, if you spend your evenings doom scrolling, figure out the cue and reward. Perhaps the cue is putting your children in bed and the reward is avoiding boredom and passing the time before sleep. The Golden Rule of Habit Change would suggest you replace doom scrolling with another activity that provides the same reward. Maybe you pick up a crossword puzzle or engage your roommate in a game of cards? Get back to the project you have in the closet? It may take a few tries, but you should be able to find a replacement if you fully understand what the reward is that you are still seeking.

Each day and schedule differs - and adjusting your break activities to reflect that is an excellent example of adaptability while still prioritizing self-care. When you look at your schedule for the day, choose activities that work for you. You may not have time for a full hour workout in the midst of your day, but maybe you have time for a brisk walk. To help reduce friction and simplify decision-making, brainstorm a list of activities you can do for short breaks (5-15 min), medium breaks (15-30 min), and long breaks (1+ hour) to make the most of this time. By having this list on-hand, you can easily select the break that best fits your ever-changing schedule.

## FLEXIBLE ROUTINE IDEAS

### Short Break
5-15 minutes

- Unplugged Tea
- Walk around the block
- Meditation (guided or self-directed)

### Medium Break
15-30 minutes

- Replicate a commute (ex: bike riding)
- Stretch break
- Hammock swinging
- Work on a puzzle
- Pet therapy
- Take time to be in nature
- Yoga
- Journal
- Adult coloring book

### Long Break
60+ minutes

- Pilates workout
- Do a crossword or sodoku
- Cook a healthy meal
- Family dinners
- Learn to paint or draw

# Playbook for Teams

Strategy #1: Write a Communication Charter

Strategy #2: Encourage Downtime

Strategy #3: Foster Authentic Engagement - Both Online and Offline

# STRATEGY #1: WRITE A COMMUNICATION CHARTER

In our always-on culture, employers expect workers to be reachable and responsive at all times. However, research shows that constant connectivity may actually be counterproductive for engagement and productivity levels.

Many employees feel compelled to respond immediately when an employer reaches out, even if communication comes after work, over the weekend, or even on vacation. Fifty-five percent of American workers reported checking their email after 11 p.m.; and 44 percent of cell phone owners have slept with their phone next to their bed because they wanted to make sure they didn't miss any calls, text messages, or other updates during the night.

Leaders can create a more positive digital culture for employees by explicitly setting the policy on when and how employees are expected to respond. Forward thinking companies, like Deloitte, are beginning to create "Team Charters" to document communication preferences and expectations. Team Communication Charters give employees the opportunity to share not only their expected working hours (which is crucial for flexible work schedules and organizations operating across time zones),

but also their preferences for how they can best be reached (email, text, phone, Slack, etc.) for different levels of urgency and what the expected response time might be. Team Communication Charters also give colleagues the chance to set scripts for how to unplug after hours and hold each other accountable.

Digital Wellness Institute

Create a Team Communication Charter by filling out the following template with the individuals that you interact with most frequently at work. Remember, this activity is a conversation rather than a contract. Use this opportunity to foster dialogue and deeper understanding of one another to improve your communication.

| | |
|---|---|
| **Team Members** | List each person on the team by name. |
| **Core Values** | Discuss which shared values can help guide how you approach your work and how you collaborate with each other. |
| **Digital Boundaries** | What are your working hours? Are there times of the day or week that you are available? |
| **Preferred Methods of Communication** | How do you prefer to communicate for… <br> - urgent messages? <br> - FYI messages? <br> - task updates? |
| **Accountability** | Consider positive means of reinforcing shared goals and examples of when exceptions might be made. |

See the following page for a full worksheet to fill out.

*Zoom fatigue is real, but in the world of remote work, there's still a time and place for video calls. Do you have protocol or a Team Communication Charter for your team to understand when you need their videos on and off?*

Instructions: Practice creating a Team Communication Charter by filling out this template with a group that you interact with regularly (colleages, family members, roommates, etc.). Remember, this activity is a conversation rather than a contract. Use this opportunity to foster dialogue and deeper understanding of one another to improve your communication.

| | | | | | | | |
|---|---|---|---|---|---|---|---|
| **Team Members** | List each person on the team by name. | | | | | | |
| **Core Values** | Discuss which shared values can help guide how you approach your work and how you collaborate with each other. | | | | | | |
| **Digital Boundaries** | What are your working hours? Are there times of the day or week that you are available? | | | | | | |
| **Preferred Methods of Communication** | How do you prefer to communicate for… - urgent messages? - FYI messages? - task updates? | | | | | | |
| **Accountability** | Consider positive means of reinforcing shared goals and examples of when exceptions might be made. | | | | | | |



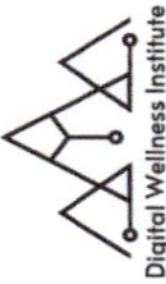

# STRATEGY #2: ENCOURAGE DOWNTIME

Amidst the constant churn of zoom meetings, slack notifications, calls, and emails, many employees feel that they lack the uninterrupted time to actually get their work done.

By actively encouraging employees to set aside downtime, employers can reduce distraction and drive long-term engagement. It's time to give employees a (real) break and, by doing so, unlock the full potential of your workforce.

## TRY IT: SCHEDULE THINKING TIME

To empower employees to be their most productive selves, encourage them to block at least one chunk of "focus time" each day on their calendars. They can even set up a short-term auto-responder explaining what they are doing and when they will be back (i.e., I'm stepping away from my email to finish this project. I'll be back in one hour). This small gesture communicates a sense of respect to other team members, but also signals that they value doing good work.

## TRY IT: ENCOURAGE PHONE-FREE BREAKS

Despite workers' desire to get away from their devices, more than half turn to their smartphones during downtime, even though research that shows that employees who take their phones on breaks feel less restored and less productive after returning to work. A 2019 study of more than 4,000 employees worldwide found that "less-happy" workers are about 57 percent more likely to spend their lunch breaks using social media, whereas "happier" workers are about 275 percent more likely to take a leisurely lunch with friends, family, or co-workers than unhappy workers are. To boost the restorative power of breaks, encourage your employees to step away from their screens. Instead, encourage them to make the most of their breaks by practicing positive habits (journaling, writing statements of gratitude, meditating, doing a random act of kindness, moving around, or connecting with colleagues) that will refuel them for the day ahead.

# STRATEGY #3: FOSTER *AUTHENTIC* ENGAGEMENT - BOTH ONLINE *AND* OFFLINE

Have you ever heard that expression, "How you do anything is how you do everything?"

In the digital age, it can be so easy to default to engaging behind a screen, but in doing so, we inadvertently ignore the human on the receiving end of the message. Make an effort to engage authentically, even if you are working remotely.

## TRY IT: WORK MORE HUMAN

- ✓ **Start your meetings off on the right foot.** Take a moment to recognize a teammate for a contribution.

- ✓ **Practice vulnerability:** Do a team check-in to get a feel for where your team is each day, and be prepared to lead by example. If you are short on time, ask everyone to say one word about how they are feeling. This exercise can give you a pulse on the mood of the group, and give you an opportunity to check in individually with team members who might be struggling.

- ✓ **Reach out:** While texting or emailing might be the most convenient way to reach out, sometimes picking up the phone and communicating with inflection can lend a more authentic connection and be even more productive.

- ✓ **Hold a virtual Happy Hour:** Consider sending you employees a starbucks gift card and starting a new remote work tradition. You can name your happy hour something fun like ConnectiviTea or Mocktail Monday!

- ✓ **Send a care package:** Send your employees a good old-fashioned care package. Employees remember employers who take care of them!

 **Create a wellness routine within your organization:** Consider a remote yoga or movement class to support team-building and physical health.

 **Offer mental health support:** Does your company offer telehealth services to support mental health? Is this information readily available? Normalize and prioritize mental health by making this information public and accessible. If you're unsure, contact HR to start a dialogue.

 **Take time to discuss personal and professional growth:** Recognize that an employee's mental health is frequently linked to their level of satisfaction with their current role. An integral aspect of Digital Wellness is a leader's effective virtual communication including the frequency of check-ins. Take the time to listen to your employees' professional goals, develop a career pathway, and support their upskilling or reskilling - in the long-run, your workforce will be more satisfied, productive, and engaged.

Keep in mind that energy is contagious and authentic engagement stems from a place of trust. If you're showing up authentically and ready to work, your team is much more likely to do the same.

Digital Wellness Institute

# Takeaways and Next Steps: Creating a Positive Digital Culture at Work



In this e-book, we have given you some concrete strategies for how to create a positive digital culture at work - one that supports productivity, raises engagement, drives recruitment, and supports overall wellness. Now that you have this information, how are you going to integrate this content and empower others?

Creating meaningful change is hard work. It might require rethinking the ways that we have always gone about business; it might mean having to rewrite policies, revisit procedures, or possibly even give up long-held practices. But if we envision a future of work that looks different - and better - than ever before, what changes do we need to make now to make that happen?

If you are ready to champion a more positive digital culture at work, here are a few steps to help you get started:

1.  **Try one idea mentioned in this book.** Maybe you want to break a bad habit and pick up a new habit. Or perhaps you want to set aside time with your team to write a communication charter. It doesn't matter which strategy you start with; just hone in on one idea, start small, and be flexible. Experiment with what works for your unique job or industry.

2.  **Upskill your workforce.** Employees are desperately seeking guidance for balancing work and home life in this unique time - conventionally known as "work-life balance." Consider offering a lunch and learn series of webinars or a keynote to introduce the concepts of Digital Wellness to your teams. By learning skills to optimize productivity and self-care in the digital age, your employees' happiness and contributions will increase in ways you never imagined. Wiley and The Digital Wellness Institute are here to support you with enrolling in your continuing education programs.

3.  **Lead by example.** Ready to create positive change? This ebook just touches on the myriad of topics related to Digital Wellness. If you are interested in helping your employees or clients embrace a positive digital culture, consider getting certified as a Digital Wellness Educator through our 10-week online program, designed to equip changemakers with tools to shift the trajectory and conversation around tech-life balance. **www.digitalwellnessinstitute.com**

4.  **Plan a company or community-wide activation.** Build motivation and spur conversation about Digital Wellness by organizing a Digital Wellness Day event. While May 7th is the official Digital Wellness Day this year, any day can be a Digital Wellness day for your organization. Download our free toolkit for ideas and inspiration. **www.digitalwellnessday.com**

Employers who choose to invest in Digital Wellness will reap the benefits of a self-aware, engaged, and innovative workforce. This could even be the key to company success. By working hard to mitigate the unintended negative consequences of technology, it is possible to help teams to flourish both online and offline.

# Glossary

| | |
|---|---|
| **Attention Economy** | A period following the Information Age, asserting human attention has become a scarce resource and valuable commodity amidst the swirl of information constantly bombarding consumers. |
| **Team Communication Charter** | A formal document that outlines your team's preferred communication methods. It helps to reduce unnecessary messages, saves people time, and improves the focus and efficiency of both team and individual communication. |
| **Digital Boundaries** | Real or imaginary lines that we draw to set expectations for our relationship with technology. |
| **Digital Citizenship** | An orientation toward online communication that includes competency in civil discourse, culturally sensitive communication, online etiquette, and information processing. A person with a high digital citizenship orientation knows about data privacy and its implication for the individual and society, is aware of how their online communication can affect others, has tools at hand to evaluate information obtained from the internet to be truthful or biased, and understands how to communicate to different audiences in a way that is sensitive to diversity and inclusion. |
| **Digital Culture** | A concept that describes how technology and the internet are shaping the way that we interact as humans. |

| | |
|---|---|
| **Digital Wellness** | The optimum state of health and well-being that each individual using technology is capable of achieving. It is a way of life, while using technology, that promotes optimal health and well-being in which body, mind, and spirit are integrated by the individual to live more fully within the human, natural, and digital communities. |
| **Digital Flourishing®** | An empowerment-oriented approach to Digital Wellness encompassing strategies for mindful technology use. This approach enables people to take advantage of the benefits of technology while avoiding associated harms, empowering them to flourish in the digital age. |
| **Doom Scrolling** | The tendency to continue to surf or scroll through bad news, even though that news is saddening, disheartening, or depressing. |
| **Nomophobia** | Also known as no mobile phone phobia, the term is used to describe a psychological condition when people have a fear of being separated from their smartphone. Other research studies define it as phone addiction. |
| **Self-Care** | The practice of taking an active role in protecting one's own well-being and happiness, in particular during periods of stress. |

# Additional Resources

**Enroll in the Digital Wellness Certificate Program**

*digitalwellnessinstitute.com*

**Take the Digital Flourishing® Survey**

*digitalflourishing.com*

**Download the Digital Wellness Day Toolkit**

*digitalwellnessday.com*

**Learn about how to upskilling your workforce at Wiley Beyond**

*beyond.wiley.com/resources*

# About the Authors

**AMY BLANKSON** is co-founder of the Digital Wellness Institute, CEO Of Fearless Positivity, and the bestselling author of _The Future of Happiness_. Her work focuses on how to cultivate happiness and well-being in the digital era. A graduate of Harvard and the Yale School of Management, she's the only person to receive a Point of Light award from two US Presidents. A sought-after corporate speaker, Amy is a member of the UN Global Happiness Council, a Fellow of the World Innovation Organization, a featured professor in Oprah's happiness e-course, and a regular contributor to numerous publications including Harvard Business Review, Forbes, and Psychology Today. Most recently, Amy was featured in WIRED's Mythbuster Series, on TED Podcasts, and on TED.com.

**NINA HERSHER** is co-founder of the Digital Wellness Institute and CEO and of the Digital Wellness Collective, the only global trade association for Digital Wellness researchers and experts. Hersher is an internationally renowned speaker and leading expert in Digital Wellness, holding a specialized MSW from Washington University in St. Louis in Norms of Connectivity and Reconceptualizing Human Development in the 21st Century. Hersher is also Founder of Evolving in the Digital Age™, a consulting firm dedicated to best practices in mental health in a fast-paced world. She holds additional credentials as an Oasis in the Overwhelm Facilitator, Teen Outreach Program Facilitator, and Meditation Teacher. Most recently, Hersher's work was in publications including The Stanford Social Innovation Review, Al Jazeera, and Voice of America.

## SPECIAL THANKS TO

Alex Gault

Sophie Janicke-Bowles, PhD.

Johnette Magner, PhD.

# About the Organizations

### ABOUT DWI

The Digital Wellness Institute exists to help organizations and individuals take advantage of the benefits of technology while avoiding associated harms, empowering them to flourish in the digital age. To that end, The Digital Wellness Institute offers a 10-week online certification program, along with opportunities for training and consultation, to support the creation of positive digital culture change.

**The Digital Wellness Institute is proud to partner with _The Social Dilemma_ (thesocialdilemma.com) in their impact campaign, changing the way technology is designed, regulated, and used.**

---

### SPONSORED BY WILEY BEYOND

Wiley Beyond helps you retain your best people, attract career-minded talent, and boost your brand. We believe that education should be more than a benefit and we're proving that by transforming tuition reimbursement and aligning talent strategy with business strategy.

# References


Robert Kraut, Moira Burke. "Internet Use and Psychological Well-Being: Effects of Activity and Audience." *ACM*, Association for Computing Machinery, 1 Dec. 2015, cacm.acm.org/magazines/2015/12/194633-internet-use-and-psychological-well-being/fulltext?mobile=false.

"The Nielsen Total Audience Report: April 2020." *Nielsen*, Apr. 2020, www.nielsen.com/us/en/insights/report/2020/the-nielsen-total-audience-report-april-2020/.

Fox, Michelle. "Remote work burnout is growing as pandemic stretches on. Here's how to manage it." CNBC.com, July, 28 2020, https://www.cnbc.com/2020/07/28/remote-work-burnout-is-growing-as-coronavirus-pandemic-stretches-on.html/.

Bourne, Vanson. "The Experience 2020 Report: Digital Employee Experience today." *NextThink*, Mar. 2020, https://www.nexthink.com/wp-content/uploads/2020/03/Vanson-Bourne-PDF-Final-Draft.pdf/.

Manavis, Sarah. "Why can't we focus during this pandemic?" *New Statesman*, May 6, 2020, https://www.newstatesman.com/science-tech/coronavirus/2020/05/how-focus-concentration-pandemic-brain-motivation-apps-pomodoro/.

Mackay, Jory. "Screen time stats 2019: Here's how much you use your phone during the workday." *RescueTime*, Mar. 21, 2019. blog.rescuetime.com/screen-time-stats-2018/.

Perrin, Andrew, and Madhu Kumar. "About Three-in-Ten U.S. Adults Say They Are 'Almost Constantly' Online." *Pew Research Center*, Pew Research Center, 30 May 2020, www.pewresearch.org/fact-tank/2019/07/25/americans-going-online-almost-constantly/.

LinkedIn.com, *2018 Workplace Learning Report*. https://learning.linkedin.com/content/dam/me/learning/en-us/pdfs/linkedin-learning-workplace-learning-report-2018.pdf

*The Social Dilemma*, Nov. 2020, www.thesocialdilemma.com/.

"2018 Workplace Distraction Report." Mar. 2018, research.udemy.com/wp-content/uploads/2018/03/FINAL-Udemy_2018_Workplace_Distraction_Report.pdf./

"The Future of Work and Digital Wellbeing." *Allianzcare.com*, Oct. 2020, www.allianzcare.com/en/about-us/news/2020/10/the-future-of-work-and-digital-wellbeing.html.

"Problematic and Risky Internet Use Screening Scale (PRIUSS)." mediad.publicbroadcasting.net/p/kplu/files/201502/PRIUSS_scale_and_guidelines.pdf./

Yildirim, Caglar and Ana-Paula Correia. "Exploring the dimensions of nomophobia: Development and validation of a self-reported questionnaire." *Computers in Human Behavior*, Volume 49, 2015, Pages 130-137, ISSN 0747-5632, https://doi.org/10.1016/j.chb.2015.02.059.

Rubinstein, J. S., Meyer, D. E., & Evans, J. E. (2001). Executive control of cognitive processes in task switching. *Journal of Experimental Psychology: Human Perception and Performance*, 27(4), 763–797. https://doi.org/10.1037/0096-1523.27.4.763

Adrian F. Ward, Kristen Duke, Ayelet Gneezy, Maarten W. Bos. Brain Drain: The Mere Presence of One's Own Smartphone Reduces Available Cognitive Capacity. *Journal of the Association for Consumer Research*, 2017; 2 (2): 140 DOI: 10.1086/691462

Neal, David & Wood, Wendy & Quinn, Jeffrey. (2006). Habits—A Repeat Performance. Current Directions in Psychological Science - CURR DIRECTIONS PSYCHOL SCI. 15. 198-202. 10.1111/j.1467-8721.2006.00435.x.

Lally, P., van Jaarsveld, C.H.M., Potts, H.W.W. and Wardle, J. (2010), How are habits formed: Modelling habit formation in the real world. Eur. J. Soc. Psychol., 40: 998-1009. https://doi.org/10.1002/ejsp.674

"BJ Fogg." Behavioral Design Center, Stanford University. behaviordesign.stanford.edu/people/bj-fogg/.

Clear, James. Atomic Habits: Tiny Changes, Remarkable Results : An Easy & Proven Way to Build Good Habits & Break Bad Ones. New York: Avery, an imprint of Penguin Random House, 2018.

Achor, Shawn. The Happiness Advantage: The Seven Principles of Positive Psychology That Fuel Success and Performance At Work. New York: Crown Business, 2010.

Toyoda, Masahiro, Yuko Yokota, Marni Barnes, and Midori Kaneko. "Potential of a Small Indoor Plant on the Desk for Reducing Office Workers' Stress". *HortTechnology hortte* 30.1 (2020): 55-63. < https://doi.org/10.21273/HORTTECH04427-19>. Web. 11 Dec. 2020.

Charles Hall, Melinda Knuth; An Update of the Literature Supporting the Well-Being Benefits of Plants: A Review of the Emotional and Mental Health Benefits of Plants. *Journal of Environmental Horticulture* 1 March 2019; 37 (1): 30–38. doi: https://doi.org/10.24266/0738-2898-37.1.30

Berman MG, Jonides J, Kaplan S. The Cognitive Benefits of Interacting With Nature. Psychological Science. 2008;19(12):1207-1212. doi:10.1111/j.1467-9280.2008.02225.x

Maccormick, Judith & Dery, Kristine & Kolb, Darl. (2012). Engaged or just connected? Smartphones and employee engagement. Organizational Dynamics. 41. 194–201. 10.1016/j.orgdyn.2012.03.007.

Duhigg, Charles. "The Golden Rule of Habit Change." *PsychCentral*, July 8, 2018. psychcentral.com/blog/the-golden-rule-of-https://psychcentral.com/blog/the-golden-rule-of-habit-change/.

Kelleher, David. "Survey: 81% of U.S. Employees Check their Work Mail outside Work Hours." *TechTalk*, May 20, 2013. techtalk.gfi.com/survey-81-of-u-s-employees-check-their-work-mail-outside-work-hours/.

Perlow, Leslie A. Sleeping with Your Smartphone: How to Break the 24-7 Habit and Change the Way you Work. Harvard Business Review Press, 2012.

Kambil, Ajit. "Creating an effective communications program," 2015. www2.deloitte.com/us/en/pages/finance/articles/cfo-insights-creating-effective-communications-program.html/.

"Less Is Not More: Forget Downsizing, Americans Are Craving More Space." Hilton.com, Nov. 12, 2018. newsroom.hilton.com/homewoodsuites/news/less-is-not-more-forget-downsizing-americans-are-craving-more-space/.

Rhee, Hongjai and Sudong Kim. Effects of breaks on regaining vitality at work: An empirical comparison of 'conventional' and 'smart phone' breaks, *Computers in Human Behavior*, Volume 57, 2016, Pages 160-167, ISSN 0747-5632, https://doi.org/10.1016/j.chb.2015.11.056.

"New Wrike Happiness Survey Reveals that Over 50 Percent of US and UK Employees Chose Job Happiness Over Paycheck Size." Wrike.com, May 7, 2019. library.wrike.com/us-wrike-hapiness-index/.

Blankson, Amy. The Future of Happiness: 5 Modern Strategies for Balancing Productivity and Well-being in the Digital Era. Dallas: BenBella Books, 2017.


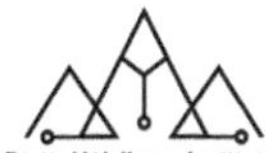

Digital Wellness Institute